In the same series by PatrickGeorge:

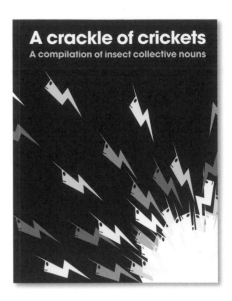

© PatrickGeorge 2012

Illustrated, designed and published by
PatrickGeorge
46 Vale Square
Ramsgate
Kent CT11 9DA
United Kingdom

www.patrickgeorge.biz

ISBN 978-1-908473-01-1

British Library Cataloguing in Publication Data.
A catalogue record for this book is available from the British Library.

Printed in China.

A shiver of sharks

A compilation of aquatic collective nouns

PatrickGeorge

A bushel of crabs

For many of us, catching a crab means hunting under rocks in rock pools or tying a piece of bacon to some string and hoping to find something bigger but in Maryland, USA, they catch Atlantic blue crabs by the bushel – a basket that holds up to 70 crabs – and fill up to 300 bushels a day.

A party of rainbow fish

Rainbow fish are brightly-coloured and live in large groups. The dwarf rainbow fish is said to be particularly social, active and amusing. Apparently if they are kept healthy and happy they will be more active and interesting to watch. Good looks and personality? Party on!

A knot of frogs
Thousands of frogs' eggs can make rich pickings for predators. The eggs of the red-eyed tree frog, however, are particularly vulnerable, hanging on the underside of leaves over water for six days to develop. Did you know that these embryos will hatch early and within seconds if threatened? Then they drop into the water below, leaving their predators tied in knots.

An array of eels

The moray eel is often considered aggressive but will only attack in self-defence. A cosmopolitan creature, it comes in different colours, sizes and patterns ranging from tattooed, speckled, striped, brown, sandy, yellow, blue… presenting a striking array of colours.

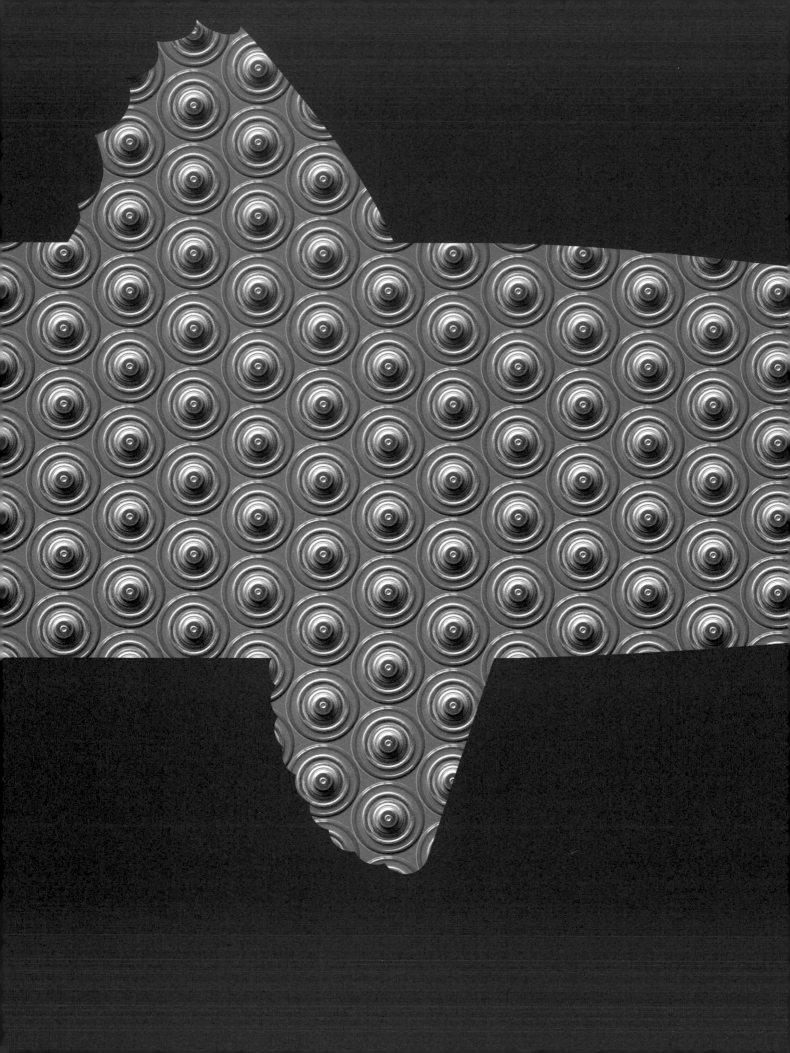

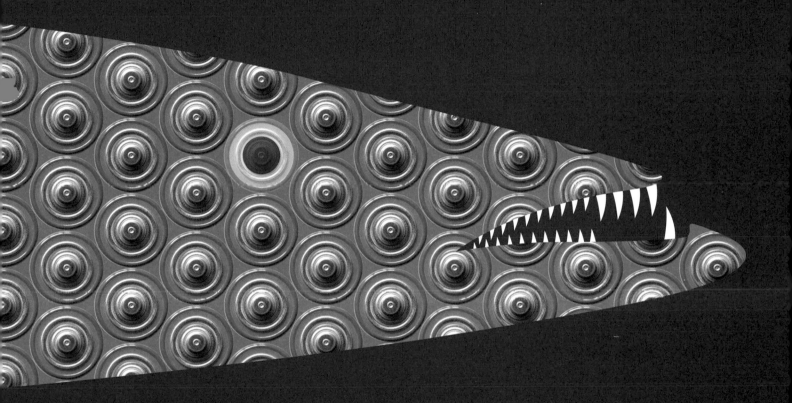

A battery of barracudas

Barracudas will lie in wait and then ambush their prey, darting out and catching them by surprise. Often drifting in a slow-moving current, they will surge out with extraordinary power at speeds of up to 25 miles an hour and will strike at anything that moves.

A turn of turtles

After a long journey to deposit its eggs, the female turtle turns back to sea. Laboriously digging its way out of its sandy nest, the hatchling then heads for the tide, juggling its fate between life and fairly certain death. The sea eagle watches hungrily overhead: "Whose turn will it be next?" it wonders.

A school of whales

Travelling in schools of hundreds, classrooms of thirty or playground pairs, some whales like to share their mealtime together before rushing out to play – noisily chatting, pec-slapping and even fighting. This gregarious, intelligent and sensitive animal is found in oceans around the world, but is sadly fighting for its survival.

A family of sardines

Google 'sardines' and you will find plenty of recipes.
It seems that the sardine makes a good meal not only
for us but for some other fish too. They spend their lives
in tight-knit communities like one big family, more
often than not ending up tightly packed into cans.

A fever of stingrays

Commonly lying inactive, camouflaged on the sea floor, this largely boneless creature has teeth which enable it to crush shellfish such as clams, oysters and mussels. And if you are unfortunate to get stung by its venomous tail, you risk suffering excruciating pain, fever and even death.

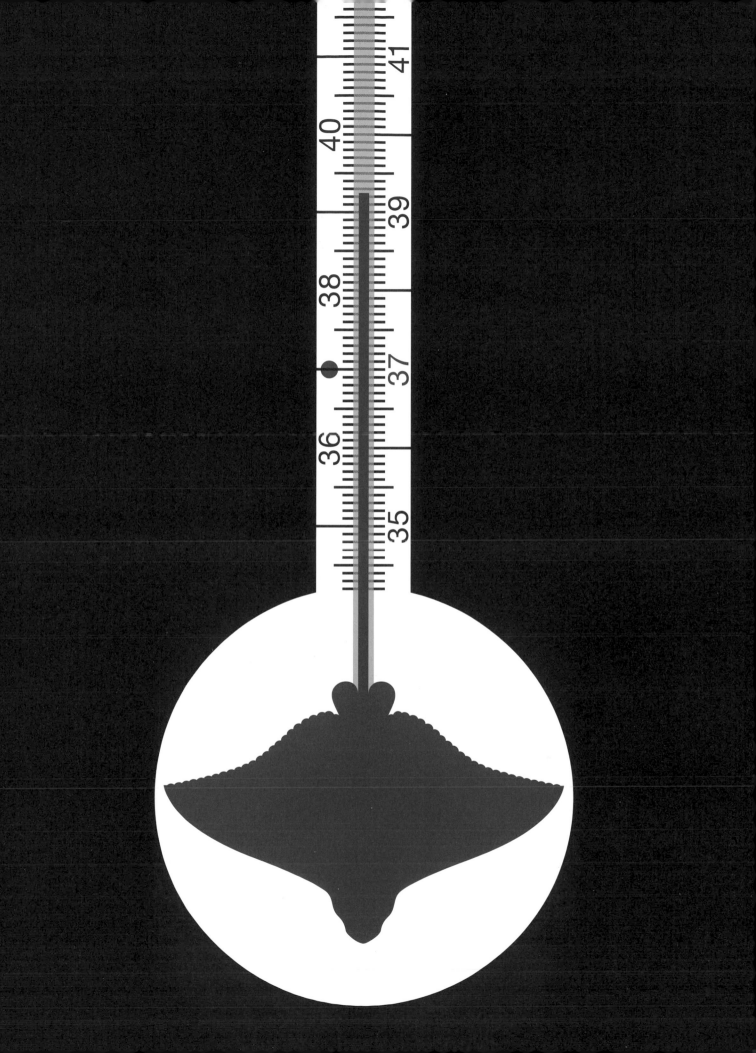

A shiver of sharks

It's easy to understand why you would shiver at the sight of a shark especially if you were face-to-face with a Great White. In fact the shark will know if you shiver in the water because it has a lateral line running along the top of its body, which senses vibrations and detects its prey.

A smack of jellyfish

A smack can sting, but to be smacked by the delicate tentacles of the diaphanous box jellyfish can cause significant scarring or sudden death. This infamous creature developed its venom to protect its fragility and will instantly stun or kill its prey to avoid being harmed by any struggle.

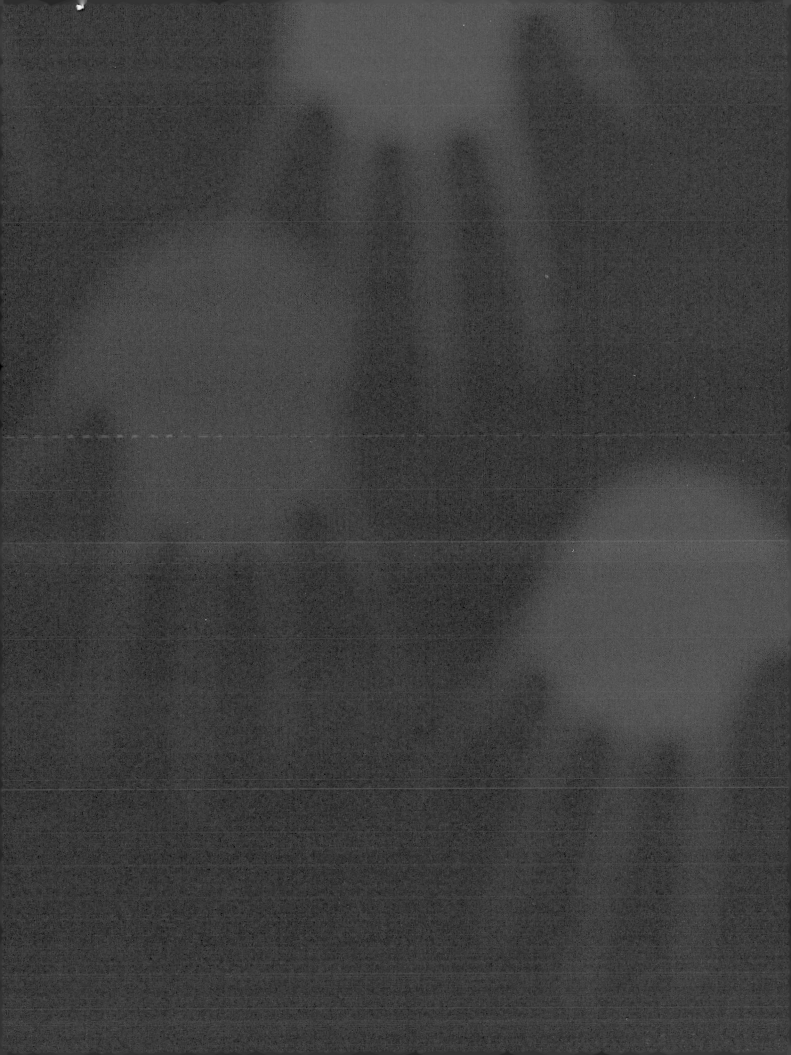

A hover of trout

Rainbow trout will hover in fast-moving water waiting
for their food to swim by but when they are the source
of food they are unusually acrobatic and feisty. If hooked
by an angler, a rainbow will often leap out of the water
again and again until it escapes or is well and truly
caught. A popular fish both for sport and the plate!

A harem of seals

The term 'harem' refers to a group of female seals in a colony – the property of one male who will fight, often bloody battles, to own them. Once victorious, he will remain loyal until the breeding season is over.

A congregation of crocodiles

You would be right to get down on your knees and pray if you came face-to-face with a crocodile. Having a virtually indiscriminate diet means that the crocodile is just as likely to eat a passer-by as a fish, zebra or bird. But this fearsome predator is also an unusually caring parent: those sharp teeth gently roll their unborn young in their mouths to help them hatch.

A troupe of shrimps

Barberpole, scarlet skunk, red rock, scarlet lady, red night, cherry, ghost and harlequin – with names as colourful as these, a troupe of dancers may come to mind… or just different types of shrimp. The 'snapping' or pistol shrimp is another great name. Using its pincers it can snap so loud that it will startle a diver or stun its prey.

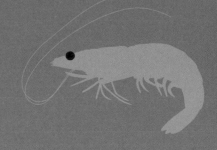

A raft of sea otters

Sea otters like to spend most of their day alone but
at night they come together to rest. They float on
their backs in raft-like formation, often wrapping
themselves in kelp, sometimes holding paws to
avoid drifting out to sea. Group sizes vary but in
Alaska up to 2000 sea otters may raft at one time.

A glint of goldfish

The common goldfish is a social and curious being that needs company and a stimulating environment. Apparently, if treated well, the goldfish will become tame, even recognising its owner and may eat from the hand that feeds it. So look for that glint of recognition and you know you're doing well!

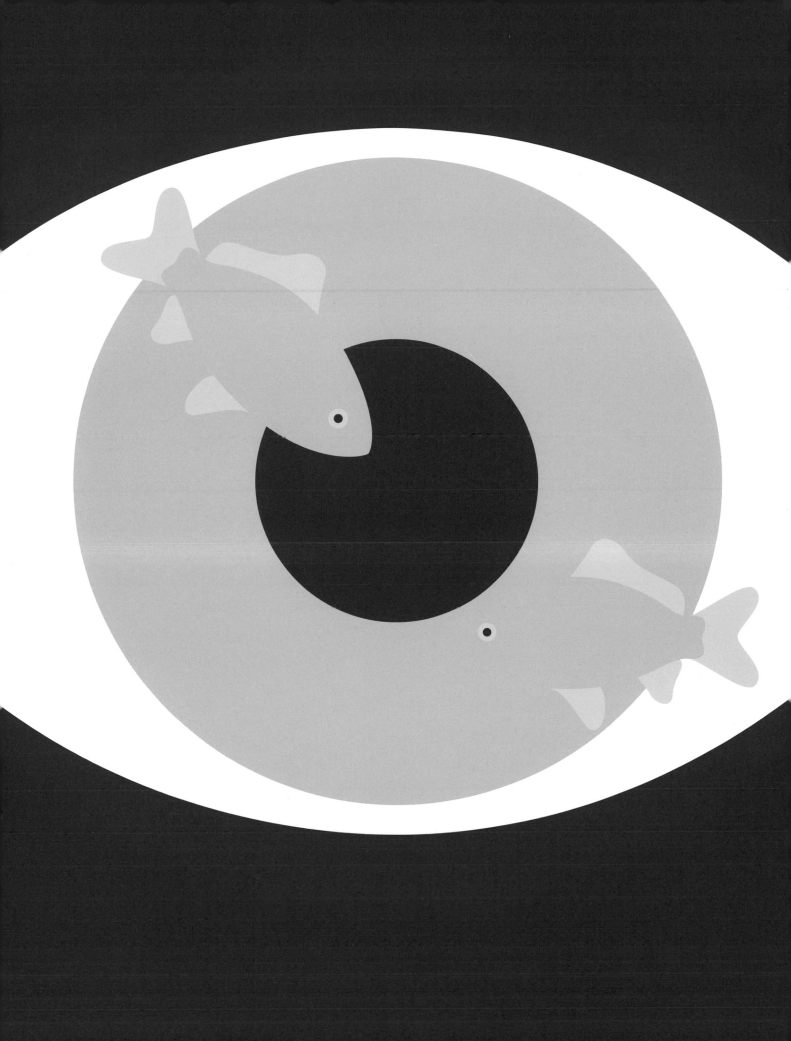

A run of salmon

Go for a run on a hot day and you might possibly
get redder as you get hotter. The pacific sockeye
salmon is silver with hints of blue and black speckles,
but once it returns upriver to spawn, its body
turns bright red and the head takes on a shade
of green. That's some long-distance running!

A pod of dolphins

This much-loved charismatic creature with its curvy smile is a social networker, creating its own music of clicks and whistles through the waves. Sociable to the core, when one is sick or injured, its cries of distress summon the others, who will help it to the surface to breathe.

A galaxy of starfish

There are well over a thousand different types of starfish. Many of them can eat and digest prey far bigger than themselves by pushing their stomach outside of their body. They are capable of forcing open the shell of a mussel to inject their stomach inside and partially digest the contents before withdrawing it again.

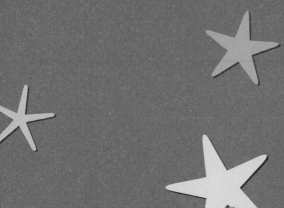
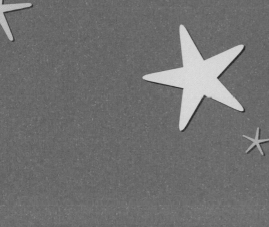